SUBTRACTION
FIRST & SECOND GRADE WORKBOOK

What Are COMMON CORE State Standards?

According to CoreStandards.org,

"The Common Core State Standards Initiative is a state-led effort coordinated by the National Governors Association Center for Best Practices (NGA Center) and the Council of Chief State School Officers (CCSSO). The standards were developed in collaboration with teachers, school administrators, and experts, to provide a clear and consistent framework to prepare our children for college and the workforce."

In order for teachers and parents to establish appropriate benchmarks for students, the Common Core State Standards help communicate what is expected at each grade level. The standards included in this Subtraction workbook are conveniently listed below for educators and parents. Using supplemental materials that support these standards will help students to achieve success at school.

The Common Core Standards covered in this workbook:

MATHEMATICS

Operations and Algebraic Thinking 1.0A, 2.0A:
Represent and solve problems involving addition and subtraction.
• CCSS.MATH.CONTENT.1.OA.A.1/ CCSS.MATH.CONTENT.2.OA.A.1
Add and subtract within 20.
• CCSS.MATH.CONTENT.1.OA.C.5 / CCSS.MATH.CONTENT.2.OA.B.2
Work with addition and subtraction equations.
• CCSS.MATH.CONTENT.1.OA.D.7

LANDOLL™

Published by: Landoll Publishing SJS, LLC.
14800 Foltz Parkway, Strongsville, OH 44149 • www.landollpub.com
© 2014 Creative IP, LLC. All rights reserved. Made in the USA.
Written by Kim Mitzo Thompson, MS Education

Cross out and subtract.

1.

$$\begin{array}{r} 9 \\ -\ 4 \\ \hline \end{array}$$

5

2.

$$\begin{array}{r} 9 \\ -\ 8 \\ \hline \end{array}$$

How many are left? ___1___

3.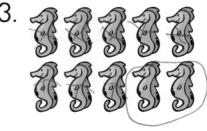

$$\begin{array}{r} 10 \\ -\ 8 \\ \hline \end{array}$$

How many are left? ___2___

4.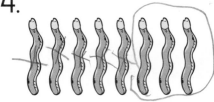

$$\begin{array}{r} 8 \\ -\ 5 \\ \hline \end{array}$$

How many are left? ___3___

5.

$$\begin{array}{r} 10 \\ -\ 7 \\ \hline \end{array}$$

How many are left? _____

6.

$$\begin{array}{r} 7 \\ -\ 2 \\ \hline \end{array}$$

How many are left? ___5___

7.

$$\begin{array}{r} 6 \\ -\ 3 \\ \hline \end{array}$$

How many are left? ___3___

Subtraction Number Sentences

Circle the correct number sentence. *Hint: Count how many in all first.*

1. Ten birds in all. Three birds flew away. How many are left?

$9 - 3 = 6$

$\boxed{10 - 3 = 7}$

2.

$8 - 6 = 2$

$10 - 8 = 2$

3.

$9 - 6 = 3$

$10 - 6 = 4$

4.

$7 - 5 = 2$

$10 - 5 = 5$

5.

$8 - 4 = 4$

$9 - 4 = 5$

3

Subtraction Facts to 10

Cross out and subtract.

1.

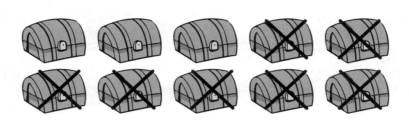

$$\begin{array}{r} 10 \\ -\ 7 \\ \hline \end{array}$$

3

2.

$$\begin{array}{r} 6 \\ -\ 1 \\ \hline \end{array}$$

3.

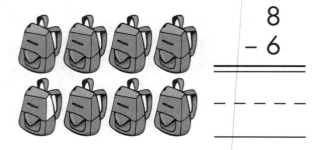

$$\begin{array}{r} 8 \\ -\ 6 \\ \hline \end{array}$$

4.

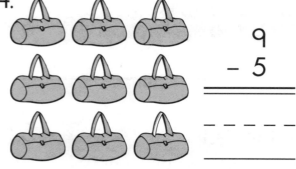

$$\begin{array}{r} 9 \\ -\ 5 \\ \hline \end{array}$$

5.

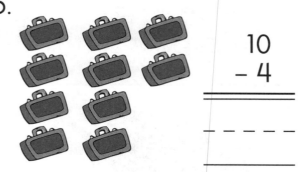

$$\begin{array}{r} 10 \\ -\ 4 \\ \hline \end{array}$$

6.

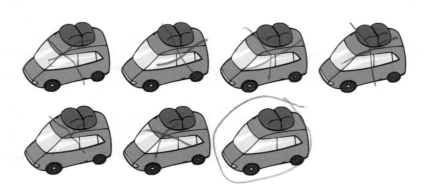

$$\begin{array}{r} 7 \\ -\ 6 \\ \hline \end{array}$$

Subtraction Facts to 10

Subtract.

1.

6	8	4	9
− 6	− 5	− 1	− 4

2.

5	7	9	3
− 5	− 3	− 1	− 2

3.

8	2	10	7
− 4	− 0	− 6	− 5

Subtraction Facts to 10

Subtract.

1.

$$\begin{array}{r} 10 \\ -\ 7 \\ \hline \end{array}$$
_ _ _ _ _
_____

$$\begin{array}{r} 9 \\ -\ 6 \\ \hline \end{array}$$
_ _ _ _ _
_____

$$\begin{array}{r} 5 \\ -\ 5 \\ \hline \end{array}$$
_ _ _ _ _
_____

$$\begin{array}{r} 4 \\ -\ 1 \\ \hline \end{array}$$
_ _ _ _ _
_____

2.

$$\begin{array}{r} 8 \\ -\ 3 \\ \hline \end{array}$$
_ _ _ _ _
_____

$$\begin{array}{r} 7 \\ -\ 4 \\ \hline \end{array}$$
_ _ _ _ _
_____

$$\begin{array}{r} 10 \\ -\ 5 \\ \hline \end{array}$$
_ _ _ _ _
_____

$$\begin{array}{r} 2 \\ -\ 1 \\ \hline \end{array}$$
_ _ _ _ _
_____

3.

$$\begin{array}{r} 5 \\ -\ 2 \\ \hline \end{array}$$
_ _ _ _ _
_____

$$\begin{array}{r} 9 \\ -\ 7 \\ \hline \end{array}$$
_ _ _ _ _
_____

$$\begin{array}{r} 8 \\ -\ 5 \\ \hline \end{array}$$
_ _ _ _ _
_____

$$\begin{array}{r} 6 \\ -\ 2 \\ \hline \end{array}$$
_ _ _ _ _
_____

Subtraction Facts to 10

Subtract.

1.

10	8	9	7	2
− 7	− 6	− 5	− 3	− 0

2.

9	4	9	9	9
− 9	− 2	− 7	− 6	− 2

3.

3	8	8	6	7
− 3	− 8	− 6	− 3	− 4

4.

10	5	7	5	6
− 2	− 4	− 5	− 3	− 5

Checking Subtraction

Subtract. Then add to check.

1.

   5 – 3 =  2 ✔

   2 + 3 = 5

2.

   9 – 5 = _____ ✔

   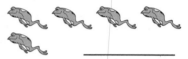

   4 + 5 = _____

3.

   6 – 4 = _____ ✔

   2 + 4 = _____

4.

   10 – 3 = _____ ✔

   7 + 3 = _____

5.

   9 – 6 = _____ ✔

   3 + 6 = _____

Addition and Subtraction Practice

$$4 + 3 = \underline{\quad 7 \quad}$$

○ 5
○ 6
● 7

Solve. Then fill in the circle next to the correct answer.

1.

$3 + 1 = \underline{\qquad}$

○ 4
○ 5
○ 6

2.

$5 - 3 = \underline{\qquad}$

○ 4
○ 3
○ 2

3.

$10 - 9 = \underline{\qquad}$

○ 3
○ 2
○ 1

4.

$2 + 2 = \underline{\qquad}$

○ 2
○ 3
○ 4

5.

$8 - 4 = \underline{\qquad}$

○ 4
○ 3
○ 2

6.

$6 + 3 = \underline{\qquad}$

○ 9
○ 10
○ 11

7.

$7 + 2 = \underline{\qquad}$

○ 7
○ 8
○ 9

8.

$9 - 4 = \underline{\qquad}$

○ 6
○ 5
○ 4

Subtraction Word Problems

Read each problem. Write the answer.

1. 4 s on the .
   3 s fall off.

   How many s are left? _____

2. 8 s on the .
   5 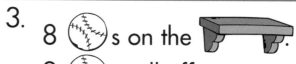s fall off.

   How many s are left? _____

3. 8 ⚾s on the .
   3 ⚾s roll off.

   How many ⚾s are left? _____

4. 6 🚗s on the .
   4 🚗s roll off.

   How many 🚗s are left? _____

5. 10 s on the .
   5 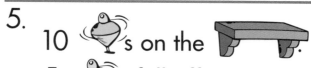s fall off.

   How many s are left? _____

Subtraction Word Problems

Read each problem. Write the answer.

1. 7 🐦 s.
   5 fly away.
   How many are left?

   7 − 5 = _____

2. 5 🐁 s.
   4 run away.
   How many are left?

   5 − 4 = _____

3. 9 🕯 s.
   3 go out.
   How many are left?

   9 − 3 = _____

4. 10 🌼 s.
   7 get picked.
   How many are left?

   10 − 7 = _____

5. 8 🍪 s.
   4 are eaten.
   How many are left?

   8 − 4 = _____

Addition and Subtraction Word Problems

Read each problem. Write the answer.

1.

4  s.

2 more s come.   How many s in all? _____

2.

8 .

4  swim away.   How many are left? _____

3.

3 s.

3 more  s come.   How many s in all? _____

4.

4 s.

5 more  s come.   How many s in all? _____

5.

6  s.

2 s run away.   How many s are left? _____

Subtraction: Sets

Subtract.

1.

15 – 8 = _____ 7

2.

14 – 9 = _____

3.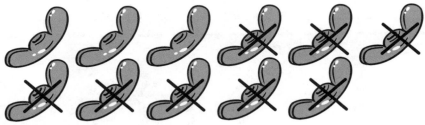

11 – 8 = _____

4.

18 – 9 = _____

5.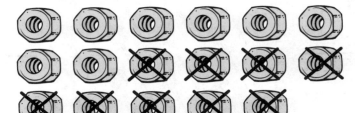

17 – 9 = _____

Subtraction: Sets

Cross out and subtract.

1.

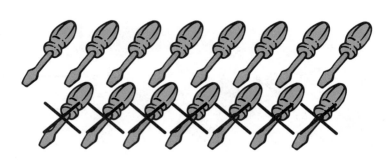

$$\begin{array}{r} 15 \\ -\ 7 \\ \hline \end{array}$$

2.

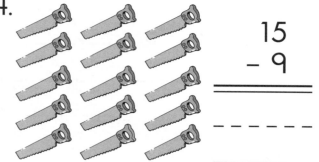

$$\begin{array}{r} 16 \\ -\ 8 \\ \hline \end{array}$$

3.

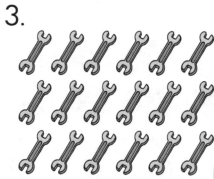

$$\begin{array}{r} 18 \\ -\ 9 \\ \hline \end{array}$$

4.

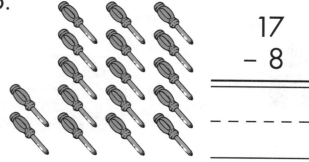

$$\begin{array}{r} 15 \\ -\ 9 \\ \hline \end{array}$$

5.

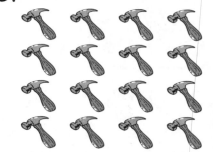

$$\begin{array}{r} 16 \\ -\ 7 \\ \hline \end{array}$$

6.

$$\begin{array}{r} 17 \\ -\ 8 \\ \hline \end{array}$$

7.

$$\begin{array}{r} 12 \\ -\ 7 \\ \hline \end{array}$$

Subtraction Facts to 18

Subtract.

1.

$$\begin{array}{r} 18 \\ -\ 9 \\ \hline\hline \end{array}$$

$$\begin{array}{r} 13 \\ -\ 8 \\ \hline\hline \end{array}$$

$$\begin{array}{r} 17 \\ -\ 9 \\ \hline\hline \end{array}$$

$$\begin{array}{r} 15 \\ -\ 7 \\ \hline\hline \end{array}$$

2.

$$\begin{array}{r} 14 \\ -\ 8 \\ \hline\hline \end{array}$$

$$\begin{array}{r} 15 \\ -\ 9 \\ \hline\hline \end{array}$$

$$\begin{array}{r} 16 \\ -\ 8 \\ \hline\hline \end{array}$$

$$\begin{array}{r} 11 \\ -\ 2 \\ \hline\hline \end{array}$$

3.

$$\begin{array}{r} 13 \\ -\ 4 \\ \hline\hline \end{array}$$

$$\begin{array}{r} 10 \\ -\ 7 \\ \hline\hline \end{array}$$

$$\begin{array}{r} 14 \\ -\ 7 \\ \hline\hline \end{array}$$

$$\begin{array}{r} 16 \\ -\ 9 \\ \hline\hline \end{array}$$

Subtraction Facts to 18

Subtract. Then match the problems with the same answers.

10 – 7 = - - - - -

15 – 8 = - - - - -

12 – 6 = - - - - -

10 – 5 = - - - - -

17 – 9 = - - - - -

11 – 7 = - - - - -

15 – 9 = - - - - -

16 – 8 = - - - - -

14 – 9 = - - - - -

14 – 7 = - - - - -

13 – 9 = - - - - -

11 – 8 = - - - - -

Subtraction Facts to 18

Subtract. Then use the code to color the quilt.

2 = red	4 = yellow	6 = blue	8 = pink
3 = orange	5 = green	7 = purple	9 = brown

1.

$$11 - 9$$ $$17 - 8$$ $$13 - 7$$ $$11 - 4$$ $$14 - 5$$ $$13 - 8$$ $$18 - 9$$

2.

$$16 - 7$$ $$14 - 6$$ [butterfly] $$13 - 9$$ $$12 - 3$$ $$13 - 5$$ $$15 - 7$$

3.

[stripes] $$13 - 4$$ $$14 - 8$$ $$15 - 6$$ $$11 - 6$$ [sun] [flower]

4.

$$11 - 2$$ [heart] $$11 - 3$$ $$12 - 5$$ [window] $$11 - 7$$ $$12 - 9$$

5.

$$11 - 5$$ $$17 - 9$$ $$16 - 8$$ [ladybug] $$14 - 7$$ [pattern] $$11 - 8$$

17

Subtraction Practice

Write the missing number.

1.	14 − ___ 6	12 − ___ 9	___ − 5 7	10 − ___ 7
2.	___ − 8 8	18 − ___ 9	13 − ___ 6	___ − 4 8
3.	17 − ___ 8	___ − 7 4	14 − ___ 9	9 − ___ 5
4.	___ − 6 3	10 − ___ 8	14 − ___ 7	___ − 6 5

Checking Subtraction

Subtract. Then add to check.

1.

$13 - 9 =$ _____ ✔ _____ $+ 9 = 13$

2.

$12 - 5 =$ _____ ✔ _____ $+ 5 = 12$

3.

$16 - 7 =$ _____ ✔ _____ $+ 7 = 16$

4.

$11 - 3 =$ _____ ✔ _____ $+ 3 = 11$

5.

$14 - 8 =$ _____ ✔ _____ $+ 8 = 14$

6.

$18 - 9 =$ _____ ✔ _____ $+ 9 = 18$

Addition and Subtraction Review

Solve the problems. If the answer is correct, circle it.
If it is incorrect, change it to make it correct.

1.

$$\begin{array}{r} 7 \\ + 6 \\ \hline 12 \end{array} \qquad \begin{array}{r} 15 \\ - 9 \\ \hline 6 \end{array} \qquad \begin{array}{r} 18 \\ - 9 \\ \hline 8 \end{array} \qquad \begin{array}{r} 8 \\ + 3 \\ \hline 11 \end{array}$$

2.

$$\begin{array}{r} 13 \\ - 4 \\ \hline 9 \end{array} \qquad \begin{array}{r} 6 \\ + 5 \\ \hline 11 \end{array} \qquad \begin{array}{r} 14 \\ - 7 \\ \hline 8 \end{array} \qquad \begin{array}{r} 16 \\ - 8 \\ \hline 9 \end{array}$$

3.

$$\begin{array}{r} 6 \\ + 8 \\ \hline 14 \end{array} \qquad \begin{array}{r} 9 \\ + 9 \\ \hline 17 \end{array} \qquad \begin{array}{r} 12 \\ - 5 \\ \hline 8 \end{array} \qquad \begin{array}{r} 17 \\ - 8 \\ \hline 9 \end{array}$$

4.

$$\begin{array}{r} 10 \\ - 3 \\ \hline 6 \end{array} \qquad \begin{array}{r} 14 \\ - 7 \\ \hline 7 \end{array} \qquad \begin{array}{r} 4 \\ + 7 \\ \hline 12 \end{array} \qquad \begin{array}{r} 7 \\ + 8 \\ \hline 16 \end{array}$$

Subtraction Word Problems

Read each problem. Write the answer.

1.

I had 11 s.

5 s popped.

How many s are left?

$$\begin{array}{r} 11 \\ -\ 5 \\ \hline \end{array}$$

- - - - -

_____

2.

I saw 13 s.

4 s swam away.

How many s are left?

$$\begin{array}{r} 13 \\ -\ 4 \\ \hline \end{array}$$

- - - - -

_____

3.

I have 9 s.

I need 16 s.

How many more s do I need?

$$\begin{array}{r} 16 \\ -\ 9 \\ \hline \end{array}$$

- - - - -

_____

4.

I had 16 s.

I gave away 8 s.

How many s do I have left?

$$\begin{array}{r} 16 \\ -\ 8 \\ \hline \end{array}$$

- - - - -

_____

Subtraction Word Problems

Read each problem. Write the answer.

1.

John had 17 s.

He gave 8 s to Ray.

How many s does John have left?

$$\begin{array}{r} 17 \\ -\ 8 \\ \hline \end{array}$$

- - - - -

_____

2.

Mary had 16 s.

She broke 7 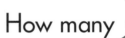s.

How many s does she have left?

$$\begin{array}{r} 16 \\ -\ 7 \\ \hline \end{array}$$

- - - - -

_____

3.

There were 12 🐰s.

4 🐰s hopped away.

How many 🐰s are left?

$$\begin{array}{r} 12 \\ -\ 4 \\ \hline \end{array}$$

- - - - -

_____

4.

Mrs. Gray's class had 15 s.

They ate 9 s.

How many s are left?

$$\begin{array}{r} 15 \\ -\ 9 \\ \hline \end{array}$$

- - - - -

_____

Addition and Subtraction Word Problems

Read each problem. Write a number sentence and solve.

1. Farmer Dan had 13 corn plants in the field. He harvested 6 of them. How many corn plants are left in the field?

$$13 - 6 = 7$$

_____

2. Tara bought 9 petunias and 7 pansies. How many flowers did she buy altogether?

_____

3. Marci picked 15 flowers from the garden. She put 8 flowers in a vase and gave the rest away. How many flowers did Marci give away?

_____

4. Keisha picked 12 tomatoes from the garden. She used 5 tomatoes for a sauce and saved the rest for a salad. How many tomatoes did Keisha save?

_____

5. Evan planted 5 green pepper plants and 9 red pepper plants. How many pepper plants did he plant altogether?

_____

6. Carlos picked 3 red apples and 9 green apples. How many apples did he pick altogether?

_____

Fact Families

Fact families are 3 numbers that are "related" and make 2 addition sentences and 2 subtraction sentences. For example — 3, 4, 7:

$$\begin{array}{r} 3 \\ + 4 \\ \hline 7 \end{array} \qquad \begin{array}{r} 4 \\ + 3 \\ \hline 7 \end{array} \qquad \begin{array}{r} 7 \\ - 4 \\ \hline 3 \end{array} \qquad \begin{array}{r} 7 \\ - 3 \\ \hline 4 \end{array}$$

Fill in the missing numbers for each fact family.

$\begin{array}{r}8\\+4\\\hline\square\end{array}$ $\begin{array}{r}4\\+8\\\hline\square\end{array}$ $\begin{array}{r}12\\-4\\\hline\square\end{array}$ $\begin{array}{r}12\\-8\\\hline\square\end{array}$	$\begin{array}{r}6\\+5\\\hline\square\end{array}$ $\begin{array}{r}5\\+6\\\hline\square\end{array}$ $\begin{array}{r}11\\-5\\\hline\square\end{array}$ $\begin{array}{r}11\\-6\\\hline\square\end{array}$
$\begin{array}{r}\square\\+4\\\hline 6\end{array}$ $\begin{array}{r}4\\+2\\\hline\square\end{array}$ $\begin{array}{r}\square\\-4\\\hline 2\end{array}$ $\begin{array}{r}6\\-\square\\\hline 4\end{array}$	$\begin{array}{r}9\\+3\\\hline\square\end{array}$ $\begin{array}{r}3\\+\square\\\hline 12\end{array}$ $\begin{array}{r}\square\\-9\\\hline 3\end{array}$ $\begin{array}{r}12\\-\square\\\hline 9\end{array}$
$\begin{array}{r}7\\+3\\\hline\square\end{array}$ $\begin{array}{r}\square\\+\square\\\hline\square\end{array}$ $\begin{array}{r}\square\\-\square\\\hline\square\end{array}$ $\begin{array}{r}\square\\-\square\\\hline\square\end{array}$	$\begin{array}{r}6\\+7\\\hline\square\end{array}$ $\begin{array}{r}\square\\+\square\\\hline\square\end{array}$ $\begin{array}{r}\square\\-\square\\\hline\square\end{array}$ $\begin{array}{r}\square\\-\square\\\hline\square\end{array}$
$\begin{array}{r}5\\+2\\\hline\square\end{array}$ $\begin{array}{r}\square\\+\square\\\hline\square\end{array}$ $\begin{array}{r}\square\\-\square\\\hline\square\end{array}$ $\begin{array}{r}\square\\-\square\\\hline\square\end{array}$	$\begin{array}{r}8\\+2\\\hline\square\end{array}$ $\begin{array}{r}\square\\+\square\\\hline\square\end{array}$ $\begin{array}{r}\square\\-\square\\\hline\square\end{array}$ $\begin{array}{r}\square\\-\square\\\hline\square\end{array}$

More Fact Families

Practice Fact Families! Write the numbers in the first two squares. Now find the third number of the fact family. Then, write the Fact Family using those three numbers.

8	7	15						

_____ + _____ = _____   _____ + _____ = _____   _____ + _____ = _____

_____ + _____ = _____   _____ + _____ = _____   _____ + _____ = _____

_____ − _____ = _____   _____ − _____ = _____   _____ − _____ = _____

_____ − _____ = _____   _____ − _____ = _____   _____ − _____ = _____

_____ + _____ = _____   _____ + _____ = _____   _____ + _____ = _____

_____ + _____ = _____   _____ + _____ = _____   _____ + _____ = _____

_____ − _____ = _____   _____ − _____ = _____   _____ − _____ = _____

_____ − _____ = _____   _____ − _____ = _____   _____ − _____ = _____

_____ + _____ = _____   _____ + _____ = _____   _____ + _____ = _____

_____ + _____ = _____   _____ + _____ = _____   _____ + _____ = _____

_____ − _____ = _____   _____ − _____ = _____   _____ − _____ = _____

_____ − _____ = _____   _____ − _____ = _____   _____ − _____ = _____

Secret Code

To find the answer, subtract the numbers, write the difference, and write the letter or punctuation mark above the correct difference below.

What Did The Math Book Say To The Other Math Book?

! $15 - 0 =$ _____

, $16 - 5 =$ _____

B $15 - 7 =$ _____

E $15 - 15 =$ _____

G $16 - 14 =$ _____

R $15 - 12 =$ _____

I $15 - 9 =$ _____

T $16 - 12 =$ _____

M $16 - 3 =$ _____

S $16 - 15 =$ _____

V $15 - 8 =$ _____

E $16 - 16 =$ _____

L $16 - 7 =$ _____

O $15 - 10 =$ _____

P $16 - 4 =$ _____

O $16 - 11 =$ _____

ANSWER

	6	11	7	0		2	5	4
12	3	5	8	9	0	13	1	15

Match The Problems

Subtract each problem. Then draw a line to match the problem with the same answer.

12 − 6 =

10 − 5 =

14 − 7 =

8 − 4 =

9 − 9 =

17 − 10 =

11 − 8 =

11 − 5 =

5 − 1 =

10 − 7 =

13 − 8 =

18 − 18 =

$$\begin{array}{r} 18 \\ -7 \\ \hline \end{array} \qquad \begin{array}{r} 15 \\ -4 \\ \hline \end{array} \qquad \begin{array}{r} 16 \\ -9 \\ \hline \end{array} \qquad \begin{array}{r} 11 \\ -6 \\ \hline \end{array} \qquad \begin{array}{r} 14 \\ -8 \\ \hline \end{array}$$

$$\begin{array}{r} 12 \\ -6 \\ \hline \end{array} \qquad \begin{array}{r} 10 \\ -9 \\ \hline \end{array} \qquad \begin{array}{r} 13 \\ -5 \\ \hline \end{array} \qquad \begin{array}{r} 17 \\ -3 \\ \hline \end{array} \qquad \begin{array}{r} 10 \\ -9 \\ \hline \end{array}$$

$$\begin{array}{r} 16 \\ -7 \\ \hline \end{array} \qquad \begin{array}{r} 14 \\ -8 \\ \hline \end{array} \qquad \begin{array}{r} 11 \\ -9 \\ \hline \end{array} \qquad \begin{array}{r} 12 \\ -4 \\ \hline \end{array} \qquad \begin{array}{r} 10 \\ -8 \\ \hline \end{array}$$

$$\begin{array}{r} 18 \\ -9 \\ \hline \end{array} \qquad \begin{array}{r} 12 \\ -6 \\ \hline \end{array} \qquad \begin{array}{r} 10 \\ -7 \\ \hline \end{array} \qquad \begin{array}{r} 13 \\ -5 \\ \hline \end{array} \qquad \begin{array}{r} 17 \\ -8 \\ \hline \end{array}$$

$$\begin{array}{r} 11 \\ -5 \\ \hline \end{array} \qquad \begin{array}{r} 12 \\ -2 \\ \hline \end{array} \qquad \begin{array}{r} 14 \\ -1 \\ \hline \end{array} \qquad \begin{array}{r} 16 \\ -9 \\ \hline \end{array} \qquad \begin{array}{r} 15 \\ -7 \\ \hline \end{array}$$

$$
\begin{array}{ccccc}
15 & 12 & 18 & 16 & 17 \\
-9 & -7 & -8 & -5 & -9 \\
\hline
\end{array}
$$

$$
\begin{array}{ccccc}
14 & 9 & 10 & 13 & 11 \\
-6 & -9 & -7 & -9 & -6 \\
\hline
\end{array}
$$

$$
\begin{array}{ccccc}
12 & 7 & 11 & 10 & 4 \\
-6 & -5 & -9 & -4 & -0 \\
\hline
\end{array}
$$

$$
\begin{array}{ccccc}
11 & 14 & 9 & 18 & 3 \\
-3 & -9 & -7 & -9 & -2 \\
\hline
\end{array}
$$

$$
\begin{array}{ccccc}
10 & 5 & 16 & 13 & 3 \\
-5 & -2 & -1 & -3 & -1 \\
\hline
\end{array}
$$

18 − 1	17 − 3	16 − 2	15 − 5	14 − 7
9 − 4	10 − 6	11 − 8	12 − 9	13 − 5
8 − 1	7 − 3	6 − 1	5 − 4	4 − 2
16 − 9	18 − 9	1 − 0	2 − 1	3 − 3
17 − 8	15 − 6	13 − 9	14 − 9	12 − 6
7 − 5	9 − 5	8 − 3	10 − 2	11 − 7
6 − 6	4 − 3	5 − 4	3 − 2	5 − 4
18 − 3	16 − 4	12 − 5	15 − 4	17 − 7
13 − 7	14 − 6	10 − 5	8 − 5	11 − 9
7 − 2	6 − 3	4 − 2	5 − 4	3 − 2

$\begin{array}{r} 11 \\ -1 \\ \hline \end{array}$	$\begin{array}{r} 5 \\ -3 \\ \hline \end{array}$	$\begin{array}{r} 13 \\ -2 \\ \hline \end{array}$	$\begin{array}{r} 13 \\ -5 \\ \hline \end{array}$	$\begin{array}{r} 14 \\ -7 \\ \hline \end{array}$
$\begin{array}{r} 8 \\ -4 \\ \hline \end{array}$	$\begin{array}{r} 16 \\ -6 \\ \hline \end{array}$	$\begin{array}{r} 17 \\ -8 \\ \hline \end{array}$	$\begin{array}{r} 18 \\ -9 \\ \hline \end{array}$	$\begin{array}{r} 15 \\ -9 \\ \hline \end{array}$
$\begin{array}{r} 1 \\ -1 \\ \hline \end{array}$	$\begin{array}{r} 10 \\ -3 \\ \hline \end{array}$	$\begin{array}{r} 9 \\ -1 \\ \hline \end{array}$	$\begin{array}{r} 8 \\ -4 \\ \hline \end{array}$	$\begin{array}{r} 7 \\ -2 \\ \hline \end{array}$
$\begin{array}{r} 15 \\ -6 \\ \hline \end{array}$	$\begin{array}{r} 17 \\ -9 \\ \hline \end{array}$	$\begin{array}{r} 15 \\ -0 \\ \hline \end{array}$	$\begin{array}{r} 3 \\ -1 \\ \hline \end{array}$	$\begin{array}{r} 5 \\ -3 \\ \hline \end{array}$
$\begin{array}{r} 16 \\ -9 \\ \hline \end{array}$	$\begin{array}{r} 14 \\ -7 \\ \hline \end{array}$	$\begin{array}{r} 12 \\ -5 \\ \hline \end{array}$	$\begin{array}{r} 13 \\ -9 \\ \hline \end{array}$	$\begin{array}{r} 11 \\ -5 \\ \hline \end{array}$
$\begin{array}{r} 6 \\ -5 \\ \hline \end{array}$	$\begin{array}{r} 8 \\ -5 \\ \hline \end{array}$	$\begin{array}{r} 7 \\ -3 \\ \hline \end{array}$	$\begin{array}{r} 9 \\ -2 \\ \hline \end{array}$	$\begin{array}{r} 14 \\ -5 \\ \hline \end{array}$
$\begin{array}{r} 5 \\ -3 \\ \hline \end{array}$	$\begin{array}{r} 3 \\ -1 \\ \hline \end{array}$	$\begin{array}{r} 4 \\ -4 \\ \hline \end{array}$	$\begin{array}{r} 2 \\ -1 \\ \hline \end{array}$	$\begin{array}{r} 4 \\ -3 \\ \hline \end{array}$
$\begin{array}{r} 17 \\ -3 \\ \hline \end{array}$	$\begin{array}{r} 15 \\ -2 \\ \hline \end{array}$	$\begin{array}{r} 11 \\ -2 \\ \hline \end{array}$	$\begin{array}{r} 14 \\ -3 \\ \hline \end{array}$	$\begin{array}{r} 16 \\ -4 \\ \hline \end{array}$
$\begin{array}{r} 12 \\ -6 \\ \hline \end{array}$	$\begin{array}{r} 13 \\ -5 \\ \hline \end{array}$	$\begin{array}{r} 9 \\ -4 \\ \hline \end{array}$	$\begin{array}{r} 7 \\ -5 \\ \hline \end{array}$	$\begin{array}{r} 10 \\ -9 \\ \hline \end{array}$
$\begin{array}{r} 6 \\ -2 \\ \hline \end{array}$	$\begin{array}{r} 5 \\ -1 \\ \hline \end{array}$	$\begin{array}{r} 3 \\ -2 \\ \hline \end{array}$	$\begin{array}{r} 4 \\ -1 \\ \hline \end{array}$	$\begin{array}{r} 2 \\ -2 \\ \hline \end{array}$

10 − 6	2 − 1	5 − 2	3 − 1	7 − 4
3 − 3	9 − 5	4 − 3	12 − 6	3 − 1
3 − 2	5 − 4	6 − 1	4 − 3	5 − 0
11 − 9	4 − 2	8 − 3	2 − 2	1 − 1
4 − 3	3 − 3	4 − 1	3 − 2	5 − 1
12 − 5	5 − 4	6 − 3	2 − 1	7 − 5
10 − 3	11 − 7	4 − 3	5 − 2	5 − 3
2 − 1	3 − 3	5 − 1	5 − 4	10 − 8
4 − 4	12 − 9	3 − 1	5 − 0	7 − 3
7 − 5	3 − 1	4 − 2	5 − 3	4 − 2